HOW BL

# Wick Poetry First Book Series

**DAVID HASSLER, EDITOR**

| | |
|---|---|
| *The Local World* by Mira Rosenthal | Maggie Anderson, Judge |
| *Wet* by Carolyn Creedon | Edward Hirsch, Judge |
| *The Dead Eat Everything* by Michael Mlekoday | Dorianne Laux, Judge |
| *The Spectral Wilderness* by Oliver Bendorf | Mark Doty, Judge |
| *Translation* by Matthew Minicucci | Jane Hirshfield, Judge |
| *hover over her* by Leah Poole Osowski | Adrian Matejka, Judge |
| *Even Years* by Christine Gosnay | Angie Estes, Judge |
| *Fugue Figure* by Michael McKee Green | Khaled Mattawa, Judge |
| *The Many Names for Mother* by Julia Kolchinsky Dasbach | Ellen Bass, Judge |
| *On This Side of the Desert* by Alfredo Aguilar | Natalie Diaz, Judge |
| *How Blood Works* by Ellene Glenn Moore | Richard Blanco, Judge |

**MAGGIE ANDERSON, EDITOR EMERITA**

| | |
|---|---|
| *Already the World* by Victoria Redel | Gerald Stern, Judge |
| *Likely* by Lisa Coffman | Alicia Suskin Ostriker, Judge |
| *Intended Place* by Rosemary Willey | Yusef Komunyakaa, Judge |
| *The Apprentice of Fever* by Richard Tayson | Marilyn Hacker, Judge |
| *Beyond the Velvet Curtain* by Karen Kovacik | Henry Taylor, Judge |
| *The Gospel of Barbecue* by Honorée Fanonne Jeffers | Lucille Clifton, Judge |
| *Paper Cathedrals* by Morri Creech | Li-Young Lee, Judge |
| *Back Through Interruption* by Kate Northrop | Lynn Emanuel, Judge |
| *The Drowned Girl* by Eve Alexandra | C. K. Williams, Judge |
| *Rooms and Fields: Dramatic Monologues from the War in Bosnia* by Lee Peterson | Jean Valentine, Judge |
| *Trying to Speak* by Anele Rubin | Philip Levine, Judge |
| *Intaglio* by Ariana-Sophia M. Kartsonis | Eleanor Wilner, Judge |
| *Constituents of Matter* by Anna Leahy | Alberto Rios, Judge |
| *Far from Algiers* by Djelloul Marbrook | Toi Derricotte, Judge |
| *The Infirmary* by Edward Micus | Stephen Dunn, Judge |
| *Visible Heavens* by Joanna Solfrian | Naomi Shihab Nye, Judge |

# How Blood Works

*Poems by*

Ellene Glenn Moore

The Kent State University Press

*Kent, Ohio*

The Wick Poetry Series is sponsored by the Stan and Tom Wick Poetry Center and the Department of English at Kent State University.

Cataloging information for this title is available at the Library of Congress.

25  24  23  22  21      5  4  3  2  1

*For Andrew*

CONTENTS

As with several of the accomplished and worthy manuscripts I pored over as judge for this esteemed contest, *How Blood Works* also stood out for its deft language, expertly rendered imagery, and sonic quality, among other mastered principles of craft that one would expect to encounter in the polished work of a poet as seasoned as Ellene Glenn Moore. However, what clearly set Moore's winning manuscript apart from the other contenders came to bear on a single word: *trope*—that often elusive yet essential quality of a collection that forms its elemental arc, a metaphorical spine that holds it together and elevates a work, transforming it into something transcendent. More specifically, as the book's title submits, the central trope of *bloodline*, which courses explicitly and implicitly throughout these pages, is masterfully employed by Moore to thread these poems together, not solely into a great book of poetry but also a powerful one that feels as alive as her heartbeats in harmony with our own.

Throughout several poems in the collection, the tenor of Moore's trope seeks to understand the emotional bloodline of family with all its given complexities and contradictions: those conflicts, secrets, transgressions, and misgivings that we inherit. Though not as evident as the color of our eyes or shape of our hands, they nevertheless circulate in our bodies' figurative blood. For Moore, in particular, that psychological inheritance comes from her parents' strained relationship in which she is triangulated. This is apparent in "Ars Poetica, 1996," when Moore refers to her father: "he sent me back to bed. I told no one because maybe it wasn't true, although I wondered who he might have been meeting there in that ocean of strange, beating night." In "Kitchens" she writes, "I open a gift from my mother: a knife. It is sharp, I know, and fine, because it is a gift from my mother." The stakes of these relationships become painfully apparent in "Blood": "He does not listen when my mother says she is flying across the country, away from our home, because she *needs this* and my father *must stay* and watch us kids while she falls apart. . . . when my mother hears what he has done, latest in this long list of cuts, she loses another seven pounds, and the three of us wait at the kitchen table, knives to our throats as we try to arrange ourselves." Then Moore bares the heart of the matter: "That is how blood works: it chooses convenience, it sinks its own ships. . . . 'Blood will out,' I yell at my hands. Baffled, they do not listen."

Moore acknowledges the universal experience of contending with one's bloodline and the struggle to let it "out" of our bodies and psyches.

However, Moore finds a counterbalance by claiming another kind of trope for bloodline, namely, art; particularly, the work of Josef Albers, which inspires a vein of seven poems that runs through the collection. These are not ekphrastic poems, per se; rather, they're homages (inspired by Albers's own homage paintings); they speak to another kind of inheritance: the lineage of Albers's art that Moore traces as another kind of lifeline to another kind of self, informing her sense of being in the world as a poet, grounding her in something other than family. For the most part, Albers's canvases are composed of bounded, rectilinear shapes; yet these shapes' colors seep into each other's edges, ever so subtly. As Albers noted: "Every perception of colour is an illusion . . . we do not see colors as they really are. In our perception they alter one another." Moore recognizes the ironic illusion of such boundaries where things divide as much as they meet, interact, and transform: "It is a meditation. Color shakes itself from the canvas, the canvas from its wooden frame" ("Homage in Crimson and Burgundy"). This echoes throughout Moore's poems in which she renders herself amid the blur of tension and harmony, with her desire to bleed through emotional boundaries, her borders of circumstances, and transcend the very limits of the body, as she writes in "Homage in Carmine and Folly": "I think of something more alive than my body, an animal with soft appendages, perched, seething itself into metaphor."

What's more, in *Interaction of Color,* published by Albers in 1963, he asserted that color "is almost never seen as it really is" and that "color deceives continually," suggesting that color is best studied directly through experience. Moore embraces these notions but applies them to the figurative colors of language: her own medium and her ultimate bloodline. Like Albers, she ponders and investigates her art; experiments with her medium's properties (memory, narrative, imagery) through the very composition of her poems in the collection: "Perhaps this is not true either, but it could have been. What I mean to say is that it happened just as the moon dipped behind the dunes, or didn't, but I do remember the moon" ("Ars Poetica, 1993"); "a flag sighs in fitful declination. It shakes off story after story. The story is never enough" ("In Paris"); and, "When I lift these memories out of night and into light 17 years away and from a different sun altogether, I do not even know which questions to ask" ("Kitchens"). But beyond all this exegesis, language is more than bloodline for Moore.

It is the very blood that flows through these pages, courses through her very psyche, as alive as her very body. The blood of her language flows into our own, her lines of poetry become our bloodline because Moore knows that ultimately "language, speaks in blood. We search its bitter grammar."

I wanted to tell you that in the gallery looping the obscene pyramidal wound of the Louvre there is a café where once I took refuge from either the sun or the rain—both extremes a kind of musculature, an oppression when the season is not right—and where my mother and I fed sparrows the fine-crumbed bread from our table. They seemed to know us, our discomfort, how the silence that followed each start displaced the easy morning like a drop of water in oil. They were unblinking, heads cocked and waiting for a tale. I read once that birds tilt their heads to orient themselves within the architecture of sound. Perhaps this has been my problem all along; no ready answer to the question of impetus, of plot. All morning we had wandered unpredictable streets, and in the Tuileries I collapsed against a painted carousel horse and finally smiled. I wanted to tell you that I ached, just ached for it to be about this: the picture my mother later taped to the fridge of me there, my circular laughter and amaranth dress—or the late sky over the river, or the light shattering itself around the watery spire of Notre Dame. Paris will always be about my mother and me, though she will rewrite this story over and over. *Your art is your art,* she will say. *It is whatever you need it be.* I wanted to tell you, but I didn't understand then what stories hold, or what they foreclose. The tale is hunger at the Louvre or streetlamps casting erratic shadows or my mother crying that I don't know how to love. Above the table in the gallery café, a flag sighs in fitful declination. It shakes off story after story. The story is never enough.

I.

# KITCHENS

I.

I cannot explain what I am doing in the kitchen so late, the house chilled and black, and I cannot explain what my father is doing here. In my thirst I have opened the fridge, alarming him to my presence. Impassive, like all dreams, he sends me back to bed and soon this night is cupped in the uncertainty of memory, the apocryphal, child-mouthed stories I tell myself when I can't sleep, when I am thirsty and the kitchen is in the opposite corner of the house.

II.

Alone in my first apartment, I open a gift from my mother: a knife. It is sharp, I know, and fine, because it is a gift from my mother. On the floor of the kitchen, I pry it from its velvet nest and run the back of a fingernail down its blade, worry the groove it leaves with my lip while the neighbors downstairs scream.

III.

I am crying again, four years old and lifted to the yellowed counters by my mother or a large woman with two names who is married to my father's best friend. Only a moment ago I was running through the long hallway on the second floor. It begins as stairs in the kitchen, rising to a door we keep open, past one brother's room, then another's, past the bathroom where my toothbrush stands to attention in a wooden rabbit with balloons painted on the side. Then a landing, a step up to my nursery where I still sleep, not in a crib but in a big-girl bed that began as a collection of walnut-stained boards but somehow became a simple metal frame with a pleated bed skirt my mother must have sewn on her iron-black hand crank Singer. My memory cannot account for the mysterious discrepancy of the bed, although when I am older I find remnants of a twin headboard and footboard in an odd storage room beneath the eaves.

IV.

I am opening birthday presents early at the kitchen table. Windows wide, summer blows in, and I tear off the wrapping paper and let it stray in crumpled blossoms across the table and floor. Books, from a cousin or an aunt. Some fantasy or adventure, one with a blue spine, and they are hardcover. I remember that: they are hard.

V.

When I lift these memories out of night and into light 17 years away and from a different sun altogether, I do not even know which questions to ask. Split in two, I hover above myself, arranging my hands into unfamiliar shapes, closing my body, putting a false name on emptiness.

VI.

Four years after receiving it in the mail, the knife is dull enough that when my mother slams the door to my bedroom, which I have offered her for the week, and I press her fine gift into my arm, it leaves a white, bloodless line but does not break the skin. For the whole week, it seems, we have bickered, my plans subjugated to my mother's vision of my life here—these groceries, that rug, this recipe she clipped from the *Times*— and it rises within us like bile as we walk up the stairs, into the kitchen where she has promised to help me but now takes offense at the way I say "There's a pen on the table" and so the door slams and the knife she has given me is too dull.

VII.

In the afternoon my friends will come for cake and tag, but while the house is still quiet, my brother and I find ourselves together at the table in a deadlock. I have left my new books strewn catty-wonk, well within my brother's angry reach, and he rears back and throws one across the table at me. It hits my arm and I am glued in place, skin smacked red and burning, and even though it hurts, I lower my chin and stare at my brother from beneath my bangs. Having expected me to cry out, my brother now wants to win. His face is blank. He lifts another book, holds it by the corner between thumb and curled index, says to me: "I have more ammo."

VIII.

One moment after the corner of the hallway cabinet reaches out for me, I am in the kitchen, no memory of what happened in between, and my mother and the large woman are coaxing a pill down my raw throat with apple juice, which I have never liked. What I don't know then but which my mother will make sure I know soon is that she never liked that woman, or her husband, my father's friend, though he once confessed his love for my mother, despite my father, and my father was incapable of making friends anyway, and isn't that so funny, so worthy of our contempt. The large woman holds my head and rocks me while I cry. Years later I imagine I can still feel a dimple in my hard forehead, a thought-line broken and dangling off the wrong way.

IX.

Soon, and for years, I will be chagrined on his behalf by this line: "I have more ammo." The false drama, the boy-ness of it. But now I am shaken from myself, and now I am outside with my mother, unable to speak through my tears as she examines the open skin beneath my eye, the blood on my chin. She scolds me to tell my friends that I "had a slight mishap" if they ask me what happened.

X.

Instead, I drop the knife on the kitchen counter, melt into the floor, press my shoulder into the lower cabinet. I am senseless. I leave a bruise on my jaw and marks on my hands, the impression of my teeth. When I examine them later, they are dark rings, unbearably small, as if they have come from the mouth of a child.

In a lower corner of the museum, past rooms
lined with bright fragments of weaponry,
armor, articulated dragon cooling his heels behind glass,
this space is inflected in shadow.
The grooves my pen makes in paper
are projected into low-relief by dim light,
while a gallery of grave, oiled pillars
heft themselves out of the silence.
They wait like tried combatants, considering
this threshold, the space
between one strike and the next, the quiet
violence that taught them repose.

# ARS POETICA

*1989*

I tell you this: the night before I was born my mother sent my waning father and two brothers down the street, elms pressing open the brick sidewalks from below, to the capitol building to watch the fireworks. Peace for my mother, and her big bellyful of me. But lights busted through the running-glass windows of our home and something in my mother—was it me, hankering to bang back?—kicked up a longing for explosion. The television made such big sounds small. Our home seemed to spire up to stars that burned in the city sky, me in the way of my mother's swollen feet as she walked up the stairs to a fire escape slinging out of a third floor window. She stepped out, sweating July iron. The ringing bars grazed her belly as she pulled us up to the gravel roof where my shuffling feet kicked over themselves. Lightbursts made my mother's face glow not just with copper, beryllium, lampblack, but now with questions, the baby ignited, bringing something hard as rock salt to a house about to explode.

*1993*

And then: when I was a child I swam with dolphins in an ocean that fanned itself across the horizon like a woman's hair spread over a pillow. I have to tell you now that this is not true, though I have seen dolphins, slipping and rolling through distant green waters. The wind pulled dune grass up from its roots. A fish threw itself onto the sand and we rubbed its scales off, offered them as a talisman to the sea, burned the body over the fire and ate until our bellies were as full as the moon's. Perhaps this is not true either, but it could have been. What I mean to say is that it happened just as the moon dipped behind the dunes, or didn't, but I do remember the moon.

*1996*

This is how it happened: my father stood in the kitchen at midnight. I did not see him until I opened the fridge and light spilled out, sliding over counters, illuminating his *hush* as he sent me back to bed. I told no one because maybe it wasn't true, although I wondered who he might have been meeting there in that ocean of strange, beating night. What I mean is that some memories turn tirelessly with the moon, some memories will not drown. When I ran from the waves in my small dreams I did not stop to study the pattern of the sand. Or, if I did, perhaps I only found the imprint of a hundred empty kitchens, handing their transgressions to the night.

# IN WASHINGTON, DC

I have walked here from my father's home,
ground littered with the carcasses of magnolia cones,
husks like shakers, bursting with seed.

\*

In the sculpture garden
grey stems arch back toward the still-low sun
and resolve into something green.

\*

Dreaming of heat, its obsessions,
carousel horses make distant children scream.

\*

All day I have been retracing my steps over brick sidewalks,
the roads sweeping away from me like unfettered glee.

\*

The sun is a muted bell behind a sky as thick as ointment.

\*

Lambskin buds, savage geese—
threatening above the winter-wracked trees,
this city is a facsimile of loss.

\*

The hydrangea
reaches out of itself,
readying a new set of expectations.

# HOMAGE IN OLIVE AND MUD

*after Josef Albers*

Tonight in the city a girl eats olives from a ceramic dish: castelvetrano, picholine, niçoise. It is love, this dish, but fragile, and her mind is deep in eddy in the darkness at the bottom of a well. She is gazing into a well. She is murmuring in the center of a field. The field is fallow, filled with possibility the well lacks—tired thing. Here, she breathes, is the ardent salt of desire.

# HAND MIRROR IN BRONZE

*Etruscan, 470 B.C.*


In the absence of language, this fragment remains:
back toward me, Eos carved
around the body of Memnon.
Her grief is its own reflection, a memory of syntax,
articulated briefly
in the luminous, cool museum light.

# JOHNNY TREMAIN

I.

I did not find out what happened to Johnny Tremain. He was a good-looking boy. Here is what I remember: cobblestones, stolen goblets, a candlelit hallway. At the bottom of the stairs, my mother flooded the kitchen with light from the refrigerator. *Why are you crying,* she whispered. The light sharpened her hands. I won't say my head was full of papers.

II.

In Chapter 2, Johnny Tremain suffers a terrible accident in which liquid silver spills from a cracked crucible and burns his hand, fusing his thumb to his palm, crippling him, I think forever. This is significant because, because Johnny is a good-looking boy. His head is empty, and now his hand is burned.

III.

In the afternoon, my father carried a box full of papers to the door and down the front steps to the street. My mother cried as she stalked through the empty house. Papers fluttered to the brick sidewalk. Johnny Tremain lived on a street with cobbled stones, in a house with empty hallways. I won't say I left my book on the rug and watched my father slam shut the car door, rub the grit from his hands.

IV.

Johnny brings home limes in a chapter I cannot remember. He got them, I don't know where. Sailors, that's right, or possibly many tented vendors along the cobblestone streets. If he stole them, I am sure he hid them in the silver goblets. I am sure he hides himself in the hallway, the kitchen, the window filled with grit.

V.

I won't say I lied when I said I couldn't find my homework. It was sitting clean on the white rug, on my bedroom floor, or maybe stuffed in the back of my desk. I won't say I put it there, half full of nothing. I pressed my forehead against the window and did not watch as Johnny's pride fell away.

VI.

I never did learn what happened to Johnny. I received a B on the final test. I won't say I hid a study guide in an empty napkin disposal can in the bathroom. My desk was empty. My head was full. When I was through, my hands were seared with graphite.

# VENISON

*for Pete*

This is how I know you, a buck's blood on the flagstone, meat parceled out, a grey knife. You pulled that deer carcass a quarter mile down the drive, chiseled something nourishing out of its remains. The patio was wet as rain, even though the summer was dry, still, the field's high buzzing carried to the table like water carried to the rocky pools of the stream. We all look for that healing balm, the trout in the river, a path cut in the field. Show me how blood changes a person; show me how to split open a body. I still know nothing of the kind of tenderness humming in your fingers when you stripped that dead thing of its final camouflage.

# IN LAWRENCEBURG, TENNESSEE

At noon in Lawrence County the earth opens,
red clay torn through, and in his casket
my grandfather is as pale as wake-robin.
I ask my father where I should sit, lean down to kiss
my grandmother who does not know who I am.
And now her hips are bothered,
her hands are saying she'd rather be anywhere
but here. We all are looking for escape—
the door, the hall—but now my father speaks,
his voice a scythe, and he says *my dad, my dad,*
and in this space even the walls are wired.
*The bees, the honey, singing in a field.*
We bare our wrists, we rock open our hands,
voices raised and falling in our laps
for we don't care to stay here long, my lord,
the cleft in the rock, this clay beneath the floor.
The clock in the hall rises over the shag,
the mud, the beaten linoleum. Did you know
your granddaddy composed songs, did you know
he fixed that clock together in the woodshop,
soft sun illuminating grit and motes,
the concrete floor thrumming beneath his feet,
the air too sweet to breathe.

# HOMAGE IN CARMINE AND FOLLY

*after Josef Albers*

The walls are blooming with mums, cascade of bitter ombre. The reddest offer no apology. A sign calls them "Reflex," blooms fisted against the cold. Much has been made of flowers with many parts—hearts, hands, mouths unfurling. I think of something more alive than my body, an animal with soft appendages, perched, seething itself into metaphor.

# SEVEN GHOSTS

*Siasconset, Massachusetts*

I.

From the roof we watch for nothing in particular—waves, perhaps, or bees looming from one collection of blooms to another. The wind shudders the grey shingles until all we can hear is the sky straining to make an impression on us. *And then what happens*—or, rather—*how is it we came to this.*

II.

Rotary: recursion, the dry pump, cobblestones. Over and over I let go of the handlebars, willing myself in circles.

III.

A streak of grass and bramble finds its way behind cottages on the lee side of the bluff. A potato moth beats windward. A weathervane contends no and no and no.

IV.

The cranberry bogs on the island's interior—moors thick with scrub pine, sand paths—almost vibrate in the evening light. This is exactly the vivid dusk I imagined, the vermillion promise that I would keep if I could only / just / remember. It is a blood offering. Sickle-feathered swallows make a great godseye above the standing water, weaving together and apart in their quest for satiety.

V.

Loom: crave, warp, that which is thrown away. Next to the bus stop, a wrought iron compass rose reaches out in a dozen directions, knitting together worlds that seem determined to drift.

VI.

In the yard, a young maple tree is just what you say. Root ball easing open, leaves pocked, new growth holding me out to the ocean. I am terrified of all this unfolding.

VII.

Leeward: point of reference, rosehips and pine, protection. Once I let a kite strip itself out of my hands and watched it grow smaller and smaller until it disappeared inside of me.

# HOMAGE IN MANY GREENS

*after Josef Albers*

Between the cattails a reedy, perverse honking asserts itself as something beautiful in the now-tired daylight. The sun declines to comment; the sun is stroking herself behind the pines. All is verdant—such a sea of cool leaves, the pond muddying the sky's clear naivety—those plump, puckering dives, the metallic grin of a mallard's back, this blade of grass, or that. The water works itself into a tizzy. The water is sick with it.

# SEEING A STUDY FOR *THE BURGHERS OF CALAIS* AT A MUSEUM IN CLEVELAND

Inside, the thin air
is as frozen as outside.
Red birds, snow crouched
like a hungry animal;
nature wonders
why we are all indoors,
backs to the wall of windows.
Nature does not wonder. It craves.
And this room,
dotted with media res instantiations
of the very loneliness swelling in my throat.
Once, my mother showed me
a bronze casting of six men
circling around themselves,
the sun seizing
dew from their arthritic shoulders,
hands steaming as if already on fire.
I moved around them,
watched as they changed before me,
spiraling, the way memory
circles me—such hunger,
their faces, red birds in snow.

## PHOTOGRAPH AT THE BRIDGE OF SIGHS IN WINTER

At one time, criminals brought here might have glimpsed
a last, broken view of light playing the water like a dulcimer,
and sighed—the Italian way—at such beauty,
astonished at their sudden loss,
this new rarity of day conceding to blindness.

*Ponte de sospiri,* they called it, the words themselves an ache
spoken into being above canal water
opaque as memory, impervious to our grief.

This is not at all about Michelangelo's *David*. The unformed figures in the gallery strain against the medium of their design. I think of them while sweaty shop windows glance by, the shapes inside as strange as the echoes of the forms of people, or this bus, or the sky gathered in glass. It is the shapelessness of these moments that inhabits me, makes me want. When I circle my own thoughts I find no sling at the ready, my eyes do not roll in warning toward anybody's hegemonic Rome. I think he must have loved them, beautiful half-abandoned expressions struggling to articulate their bodies through every level of space, grasping their faces as if stone might truly brook their elemental rage. I think he must have loved them too much to let them rest.

II.

# BLOOD

I.

In summer I count the scratches on my arms. Seventeen. Twenty-four. Nine. I don't know where they come from, then or now. Perhaps my bike, or the leprous bark of the hickory at the corner of Pitman and Coffin. Once, as I stand on the pedals, my bike skids out from under me and shoots across a slick of sand scattered over the asphalt. From my back, I cannot tell if I am lying still or running headlong into the sky.

II.

Run from the slope, I am stopped by a tree. This is how one of the Kennedys died, my mother reminds us all, and she asks my father why he wasn't with me. The doctor pulls a silly face when he puts his hand in my puffy snow pants. He wants to make me laugh while he feels the bones for a break, but he has his hand in my pants, which is not at all funny, only necessary, which, at five, I believe I understand. But I know there is nothing wrong with me. No breaks, just blood under the skin, a continent rising in my hip.

III.

This is what my mother says: after she broke the news of her third child, me, to her parents-in-law, my grandma—small grandma, biscuit grandma, lying on the couch grandma, pleated pants up to her waist grandma, clipping strangers' obituaries to send to my mother after the wedding grandma—asked my mother if she had considered an abortion. This is a strange thing for a mother to tell her daughter. I am talking about myself. I wonder about the context. But I know what happened next. For years my grandmother called me "sweet little angel girl," and I tore down all of the laundry in the yard and bled when my brother threw a new book at my eye the summer I turned eight.

IV.

Home from college, now the lid of the toilet is broken, porcelain so sharp that though my knuckle barely brushes its fine edge as I reach for the hand towel, a clean split appears, as clean as parted legs at first, and then a sudden welling up. I hardly feel a thing, but light-headed in the kitchen I say, "Something happened," and my brother pulls my hand under cold water, fills the split with dish soap, cleans my blood from the sink.

V.

He does not listen when my mother says she is flying across the country, away from our home, because she *needs this* and my father *must stay* and watch us kids while she falls apart. He cannot stay and so for the first time he coaxes his parents up from Alabama. Grandma's blood pools in her feet on the plane, and they stay in this house while he is in Egypt or Russia with someone we haven't met yet, and when my mother hears what he has done, the latest in this long list of cuts, she loses another seven pounds, and the three of us wait at the kitchen table, knives to our throats as we try to arrange ourselves, but what did she expect? What did she expect?

VI.

Cutting onions for my mother's smothered chicken I slice the pad of my finger, the longest one. She wraps it in paper towel, takes a call on the landline, shutting its curlicue wire in the backdoor when she leaves to sit on the stoop. This is like when she and my father talked on that stoop, only now he is a phone. Or, he is a lawyer on a phone. No, he is a wire shut in a door. Inspired, I take a red marker to the paper towel, as though I have bled through, hold it to the window and watch my mother's jaw drop. "I'll call you back" is, maybe, what my mother says.

VII.

What did I expect, rummaging through that desk in Florence, Alabama,
photograph of my college father, that stone building behind him like a
bloodless face? I have to draw the line somewhere, maybe cut back on
things my mother says. In another story I am not born in summer, my
mother does not run up his phone bill or put a doubtful hand on her
hip when my father suggests they share a home to save money. That is
how blood works: it chooses convenience, it sinks its own ships. I see I
have his jaw, that blank college stare. "Blood will out," I yell at my hands.
Baffled, they do not listen.

III.

Ten feet from where I sit, the light moves across the coral flagstone in a steady march toward the ocean. The ocean's bones are fan and fire, plaintive things asserting themselves in a mass of pointillism and soft hashmarks, like an art student struggling to get down the meticulous way the light leaves grooves in the water, or how the distant and fernlike trees are gathered and compressed to a single point. In Brussels or Florence, my mother is filling a jar with water and rolling up her brushes. She is forming a language with her fingers, the city wound up and ready to be released. It is no accident that the farther objects travel from me, the closer to each other they appear: the grey sea of olive leaves whose curves and flickers she followed with a pencil, the bright tenor who sang in the study, my leap to help him when he seemed to forget the words. I am always reaching for the words. In summer I pluck inedible apples from a tree by the ocean, I sprawl on the buckled floor and study a game carved inside a wooden orb, spry horses of many colors chasing and chasing each other around the curvilinear core. Like all approximations, this is about perspective. The sun intensifies as it shrinks; the sun grows to a point.

# HOMAGE IN GOLD AND GREY

*after Josef Albers*

A runner splits the light, making a path along the river by a windblown tabebuia. The tree scrambles itself into mouthy trumpets, heralding the runner's sweat and breath. The light makes its own meaning. It inhabits the space carved by the runner, the tabebuia, the river saturated in its own thoughts.

# WHALE WATCHING IN EARLY SPRING

### I.

We weren't expecting this drought, the coolness
of the morning lacing its fingers through the afternoon,
the road crisp as an apple peel. We follow one clean
turn after another, stop in a field scooped from powerlines.
It's a rocky strand, plump with strange seals,
the sound of sky bearing down on us. The rocks, oxalis,
the ruddy path. We are gasping for distant waves, the wild
air, unsure of our place between sand and pine.

### II.

I make you sit behind the wheel while I examine
a dusty berm brimming with rosy-headed succulents.
This close drop into cold water, tender mustard
blossoms, full pine, that sweet-smelling ache.

### III.

Once, we think we see a whale breach,
a thought surfacing, rolling into expression.

### IV.

I am no mountain,
I am no open sea.

# HOMAGE IN SAP AND GRANITE

*after Josef Albers*

Lichen sprouts from the beaten stone, making a map of itself, fractal globe from which we watch the pine trees siphon mist into parallax. The forest doesn't understand our stories—what we will do about the house, why the hedge won't grow, how we will raise our children. Protected by the outcropping, a cache of small tokens—leaves in brittle colors, a bit of green glass, a notepad but no pen. The mist funnels the receding pines. We resign ourselves to egress.

# A TRADITIONAL SCULPTURE

*after Eleanor Antin*

I am observing the blue line
gather itself into constellation,
imagine itself red, pink, green, white.
It seems to be reaching toward me,
while just a few rooms away a woman carves her body
and exacts from the medium something
cruel, not a layering on.
I am telling you these things
because I, too, am hoping to find pain,
a beast, a house—already designed, waiting
for the carver (I am the carver) to nod in admission,
to articulate the form without a gathering,
a building up, an addiction.

# AT BIG CYPRESS NATIONAL PRESERVE

In a clearing we find the woody stems of cabbage palm
are quick-burning things.

*

All afternoon we see to the fire, feeding fronds
to its burning belly,
our want thicker than the smoke
that splits the light.

*

All afternoon I have been looking for bears,
waiting for a black head to rise in the distant hammock,
grass burned blue beneath the falling sun.

*

We follow a path pressed into the field,
as though we are bobbing in a following sea.

*

A rash of inland birds release their cries.

*

All afternoon we have followed the murmuring
map of insects carved in our firewood.

*

Hissing like fat, releasing steam,
the wet logs make beasts of themselves.

# IN SANTA BARBARA COUNTY

In a field stolen between those mountains, poppies,
flaming in dusk, beg to be worshipped.

The mountains bristle, egos too fragile in all this heavy light,
this light tactile, full as a peony pregnant with color
and about to break open.

The mountains hang in a picture over the bed—no, a window—
and rosemary in the garden, a prickly kind of grace.

I hardly know how to name it all—the high-water mark etched into shale,
the scrub on the mountain, that sweet-faced little flower
crowding the road north—

*oxalis,* it's called—there—*oxalis.*
It is a stone I roll in my mouth to ease the sensation of thirst.

# HOMAGE IN CRIMSON AND BURGUNDY

*after Josef Albers*

I am trying to convey the big emotions—ecstasy, doom. I am looking at neither the wall nor the red bowl awash with intention, crushed berries, euphoria, that plush stain. It is a meditation. Color shakes itself from the canvas, the canvas from its wooden frame. The bowl is like a puncto from the corner of the room. It is aggressing. It attends.

# BEDROOMS

I.

As a child I come to my mother's room at night, seeking a comfortable body, a closet clear of monsters, a different kind of darkness. It is the darkness in the hallway between us that frightens me the most—no windows, alive with its own pulse. I cannot see my fingers in front of me, as though my body were receding into nothing.

II.

In the small hours of the morning I wake Andrew and ask him to roll me from my right side to my left. Some slight motion has thrown my back and now my body won't turn when I tell it to, medical emblem of more nuanced misgivings about my ability to find grace in movement. I think of a story my mother tells: pirouetting across a stage in San Francisco, air disarticulated around her body, which she moves with the sort of trust I have never been able to muster in myself.

III.

Unconscious, my body renews itself without my numb interventions. Light from the windows makes the bedspread glow, and in this halo I am pulled from wakefulness into the bodily machinery of sleep.

IV.

I slip under the covers in my mother's bed, just a moment ago awoken by a helicopter outside my window—no, an engine under my bed—no, the air conditioner—and as she puts her arm around me she says, "You're so small, there's hardly any of you there." She says it with something like awe, tenderness, my body not quite something to be admired but something to be petted, something to yield.

V.

In her story, the actor at the other corner of the stage is flirting with some body in the wings and fails to catch my mother's swirling form. She tumbles over the footlights, wrenching her back, and it will never be put quite back in place. All I have done is sit up out of bed strangely and my body rebels against my clumsiness. Better to stay in bed, it says, than to use me the way you do.

VI.

Strange to think that my body makes itself without my knowledge— breath to blood, blood to lymph—the circuits and turnings I cannot feel or taste except as they gather presence, like a wave reaching the shore. I cannot see where the wave begins, which lonely wind swept it up, which sea-bottom grain of sand held back its foot until it grew large and unruly, falling over itself in a clamor for the distant dune grass. I adjust my arm under the pillow, I grow new skin, I wake with the sun, but I am utterly absent from myself, like the sunburnt canopy of leaves that spares no breath for a bead of water wicking through a tender, white root.

VII.

Held against my mother's body, I sleep. In a few years, in my own bed, I lie on my back in lamplight and look down between my small breasts to my belly. How new it seems, and frightening, no longer a bowl carved between my hip bones. I lift my hips and lower them, consider them this way and that, wondering if I ought to wish there were more of me, or less.

VIII.

Or, perhaps I am growing larger, swallowing the darkness, the hall, our bedrooms, until my body is itself a house and I am slight inside of it, feeling my way along the walls.

# MIRROR WITH HANDLE IN THE FORM OF A FEMALE FIGURE

*Etruscan, third century B.C.*


Here, a woman is made
to be held and behold, both
object and subject. Over and over
she lifts her hand to her lips
as though she could draw words from her mouth
if only metal might yield. Close to her side,
a vial of scented oil. Once, she may have said more
than the globe above her head—now,
we are all simply watching.

# HOMAGE IN ONYX AND BLOOD

*after Josef Albers*

I don't know who first accompanied me into the copse of bleeding dragon trees, limbs thick and bent black against the afternoon swell of clouds. Mulched ground opening under our hands like flames, rain smell turning us toward a memory of big water. Even the trees reach toward desire, longing for a body of their own. Stem open, emphatic sap, bark splits—astonished, it abjures language, speaks in blood. We search its bitter grammar, we follow one hand with another. We move under limbs that undulate with oceanic aspirations.

# IN CHICAGO

Outside the museum, thin branches harbor painfully red berries, and after hours on foot in the city my small toe is twinging again, phantom of a fracture I can hardly remember, vestige of my walking madness in a still apartment during the sharpest spring I ever swallowed. In winter, thirst is different—empty, a withering smallness. In a café, a man smolders, gestures his malcontent across the wide table we share, and tells me he's not one to play with. Traffic on Michigan Avenue seeps by in fits and starts, like frore water channeling down a window. Somehow the sun has abandoned the frozen sky on the other side of the city, while I have dwelt on trivium that has swelled to the size of a skyline. In a few moments, I will meet an old friend on the northwest corner of Adams and Michigan and I will disappear into her car, and while there is no mercy in the last notes of this blue hour, there is drinking in a stark neighborhood in the Loop and a crack about my mental faculties. Clément Première Canne doesn't make me remember or forget. I'm not talking about the man in the café, who is also not thinking about me, will also never answer my baiting emails that are about as veiled as the winter sun. Now I've had to sip the caustic tang of bromide. *I wish I could forget you,* I want to say. Which is to say I looked for you without reason when I went to put my hair up in the bathroom, sat alone at the table, walked in the night for ice cream I could not finish in the cold, which seems apropos of this particular emptiness.

# ARS POETICA

*2010*

And then: an old man and I looked through the scrap pile in the back, sifting through lonesome reams of brake pads and spools of cable housing, orphan top tubes, wheels, tires deflated and folded over themselves like cordgrass bent beneath the bellytrail of some slow bayou beast making its way to the river. Hefting a half-built bike up to the steel stand clamp, the man said *There's only one rule: Don't let the levee bust.* Beneath his white face a longing, something thick ebbing between us. He kept a bum hand in his pocket, hobble-tripped to a bin damp with river and leaking viscous oil. The bike's naked wheel spun in air sliced with a fan's sharp and rollicking breath. Plumes of dust eddied in the river-soaked light, flooding our hands with nothing we could hold.

There: at mile twelve we stopped at the chattering of some small trees, distant against the low sky doubling itself across the shallow waters of the swamp. *What kind are they?* I asked. *Ibis? Egret?* Heavy in the brush, an alligator grunted. We phosphoresced in the noon sun, praying with small breaths, hot, feathery seeds sticking like tattoos to the sweat on our necks. In a heave, then, the trees split open, releasing a hundred white slips into the sky. The empty branches hunkered down as though for sleep, horizon printed with saw grass, bromeliad, the bleak thumbs of cypress. We shivered in the sun, thickened our breath, pressed our pedals forward like a heart beating beneath bone.

You tell me this: the inlet was not carved from this spit of land by glaciations, frozen inching of big water. Not the insistences, waves, the riving wind-limned eye of a storm. But rather, the steady press of man, his mechanical arm cutting through the thinnest slip of sand between cities. No more natural than this causeway, fit in steel and concrete, upon which we now pause. Great skeins of standing water plait and unplait themselves beneath us, negotiating this twin-mouthed threshold, open to the ocean and the buoy-studded bay. And still, the sun lights the water, the sluiced rocks, and from this glassy stretch of rain-damp road we can almost taste the night. Low in the waterlocked sky, the sun sounds like a first note in a dimmed theatre, wavering in tremolo before breaking into pieces.

## TRYING TO CONCEIVE IN SUMMER
## IN BURGUNDY

In Beaune I learn that chalk in the terroir
makes the wine creamy, while a man
who has walked the vineyards all day, feeling the ground,
rubs thick mold-fur from a crisp, aventurine bottle.
I have to sort myself out in this thirsty smattering
of summer rain. Everywhere the earthworms
are making excruciating time across the pavement,
beech trees shrugging off an anxious light.
The gutters make monsters out of such small water.
Late at night and pied-eyed on a middling Côte de Nuits,
I work myself over in frustration, stewing like stem and tannin
in our lack of liquidity, fear of wasted time,
that sinking feeling of not having fun the *right* way.
I understand that I am talking to myself
the way my mother talks to me.
To muddy the theme, my parents traveled
these same molten roads in their youth
and now in the vicissitudes of age and separation
each has claimed that memory as entitlement.
To muddy the theme, my friend has just had a miscarriage,
which the nurses have termed a *chemical pregnancy,*
as if her hoarse voice over the phone, the terror between her words
were simply a technicality. I see that I am no deep pool.
I understand that the heavy clouds over crystalline-gold grass
are trying to tell me something vital, that I am on the banks
of my own self, unsure of where to step, or if I am meant
to ford at all, to cross in some distant and holy sense. I am too married
to ground I've already left, too afraid of my own pleasure,
these delicious anthologies: the vintner in the cellar, his sweet
lollygagging dog and grandmother in slippers,
the frighteningly blue sky composing itself
in an instant—
and again—
and again.

# EVENING AT THE NATIONAL CATHEDRAL

I.

When I come in I dip my hand in the holy water, as I have done a hundred times before. Now I am sitting in the same wooden chapel chairs of every Friday of every school year, watching dusk light percolate through the stained-glass windows as I sink into evening. I have walked miles in the rapturous cold, pressing against this anemic ache. The blond wicker and twill seats are a balm. I was a child the last time I sat here, or ran in circles around the flagpole on the green, or recited poetry in the Bishop's Garden.

II.

In our Cathedral-approved white chapel dresses, we can easily discern who has graduated from undershirt to cotton training bra to the thin-strapped satin our mothers wear. We've learned about puberty and periods in health class, and in the lunch line a classmate has just asked if I've started mine. I haven't, although her tentative question tells me that she has. I am seeing my face change in the mirror. Now in the warm light our bodies are bright against the stone. We lift our faces and sing.

III.

One year ago, due to depressive inability to accomplish simple errands (make an appointment with the gynecologist, drive to the pharmacy) and a long-standing but habitually repressed thought (*what would my body be like . . . ?*) I stop taking my combination estrogen-progestogen oral contraceptive pills. Suppressed ovulation, thickened cervical mucous, artificial blood. From adolescence, my body has suffered 144 meaningless menses.

IV.

Just before the south transept, where once in the balcony I sang "In the Bleak Midwinter" beneath the now-fading Te Deum window, I nurse my exhaustion: joints watery, lower belly dully aware of its own emptiness. There is more blood than I've come to expect these last months. Twice already I have bled through my undergarments, with nothing to do about it but exhale and proceed. My body insists on becoming part of my vernacular.

V.

Years ago: I have a dream I see my daughter, not yet made, here in this holy space. Her white dress grazes her knees as she tips her own wooden chair against the stone piers, marveling at the light diffusing through the great Rose Window. Her eyes wander like incense.

VI.

My body changes, it seems, immediately. In the absence of cycle-defying hormones, my thighs and hips shrink, the ribs that splay from my sternum announce themselves, my face makes itself a shade slimmer. I think of the adolescent months following that first prescription, clear-skinned at last but still fraught: my brother ridiculing the slight paunch spilling over my after-school-sports uniform, my mother intimating to me how much like a dancer I *used* to look. Everybody makes a claim. I never thought of my body so much, until it wasn't mine.

VII.

Once, I nestled in these choir pews and raised my voice. Above me, faces emerge from the stone and every corner holds a figure. Dim sunlight from the clerestory throws a clot of color into the nave. It melts across the limestone walls as the sun sinks. Everywhere I look I have already looked; everywhere I stand I have already stood. Something has been taken from me.

VIII.

Ovulation suppression, I learn, can outlast the final dose of hormones by months. I am indignant when I realize this. Already I have been revisited by the ghost of adolescent acne that set me on the pill in the first place, and now I can't even menstruate like an adult.

IX.

I start my period the summer I turn twelve, and immediately I am initiated into the strictures of womanhood. Keep your products close at hand but concealed. Don't make it into a *thing*. Check your bathing suit for tampon strings. Roll used pads in toilet paper to hide in the trash. Soak stained underwear or sheets immediately, and use cold water because hot water sets blood. Don't wear white. Carry spares with you to avoid embarrassment. Don't be embarrassed.

X.

A doctor tells me that I don't want what I want. *I have questions*—she tells me, "no, you don't." *Some of my friends*—she tells me, "uterine perforation" and "contraindicated for nulliparous females." *Well, according to my research*—she tells me, "yes, there was a time in my life when I also didn't care about my body." I haven't had my period in nine weeks. I don't want to return to hormones; I want to try a copper IUD. No, I don't need her to administer a pregnancy test. Because I'm not pregnant. Because I know I'm not. Because I'm learning my body, I am paying attention, I am listening, and I know. Better than her, I know. For the first time, I know, I know.

XI.

Longing makes its own syntax, builds its own cities around a wellspring of loss. I partition it off, erect temples to trauma and possibility. The buttresses and piers cascade like bundles of wire, cables of stone packed for structural integrity, striations of mortar plummeting to the marble floor.

XII.

Fridays, I stand in a white chapel dress and immerse myself in ecclesiastical nostalgia. I am aware that I am on the cusp of becoming. I hardly know what to do with my chest, my stomach, that unappeasable yearning to be filled with things that have never happened. No one could be ugly here. I want to melt into the windows, agitate myself apart until nothing but color remains.

XIII.

The first time I have my period as an adult is a revelation. Here is real blood, more real than the withdrawal-induced bleeding that followed each 21-day regimen of medication. More real, even, than the taste of iron in my throat when a cough blows through my body, or the crimson line beading up on my skin when a nail catches my arm—a native response to the dips and rises of this geography, absent intervention or invasion. I am relieved my body knows how to do something without my having to plead.

XIV.

The stone is singing now in wind that whips between the towers and the buttresses. It fades in and out behind the chatter of the choir boys. The Cathedral is vibrating, threatening to break open into song, intoning like water through a dam, a gorge, insistent and low, full of deep color and eddying around my consciousness, or I around it.

XV.

Unmedicated, I feel everything: the man with the cap and stubble in the checkout line, the couple holding each other on the sidewalk, the waitress touching my fingers as she hands me my card. Two months since my cycle returned and I am still dazed by the flux of desire and loss. I stare at myself in the mirror. I touch my skin. I am startled by my own incandescence.

XVI.

At this hour, the mottled color staining the limestone and marble nave looks as though it might have emanated not from the windows, but from the stone itself. As though light could live inside stone. As though in its struggle to emerge, it might have shattered into brilliance.

~

## DRIVING THE BLUE RIDGE PARKWAY
## ABOVE ASHEVILLE

This is a different kind of deliverance;
not from circumstance, but from ourselves.
Winter light turns the bare-boned trees into quicksilver.
Everything important rises to the top—the early leaves,
white bone of a deer carcass cresting in a hollow,
peering through the limbs of the just-budded rhododendron
to watch water plunge through the gorge
like everything tender and fatal coursing between us now.
It echoes, in this thin air. None of this is spontaneous.
It is incessant. It cuts its path.

## ACKNOWLEDGMENTS

Grateful acknowledgment is made to the editors of publications in which these pieces first appeared, sometimes in earlier versions:

*Alexandria Quarterly:* "Driving the Blue Ridge Parkway above Asheville"
*Bird's Thumb:* "In Santa Barbara County" and "Venison"
*Brevity:* "Blood"
*Caliban:* "Homage in Gold and Grey," "Homage in Carmine and Folly," "Homage in Onyx and Blood," "Hand Mirror in Bronze," and "Seeing a Study for *The Burghers of Calais* at a Museum in Cleveland"
*Chautauqua:* "Johnny Tremain"
*Cordella:* "A Traditional Sculpture," "Mirror with Handle in the Form of a Female Figure," and "Bedrooms"
*Fjords Review:* "Kitchens"
*Jet Fuel Review:* "1996"
*The Journal:* "Homage in Crimson and Burgundy"
*Kingdoms in the Wild:* "Homage in Many Greens"
*Lake Effect:* "Photograph at the Bridge of Sighs Winter"
*Ninth Letter:* "1989"
*Poet Lore:* "Trying to Conceive in Summer in Burgundy"
*Raleigh Review:* "At Big Cypress National Preserve"
*Salamander:* "2010," "2013," and "2014"
*Scalawag:* "In Lawrenceburg, Tennessee"
*Spillway:* "1993"
*Swamp Ape Review:* "Seven Ghosts"
*A Velvet Giant:* "Evening at the National Cathedral"

Some of these pieces appear in the chapbook *The Dark Edge of the Bluff* (Green Writers Press, 2017).